All About
Electricity

by Melvin Berger
illustrated by Marshall Wilborn

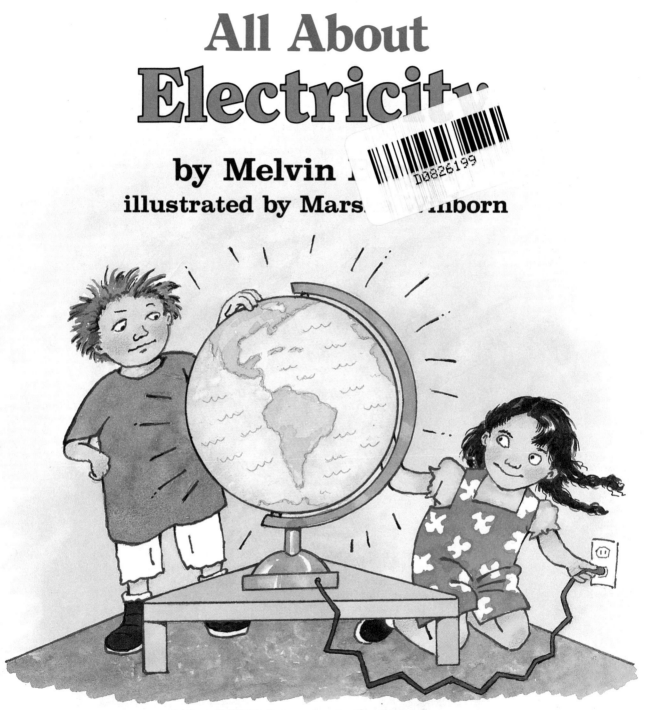

SCHOLASTIC INC.
New York Toronto London Auckland Sydney

For Matty
— M.B.

With thanks to Alberto Bianchetti,
Niagara Mohawk Power Corporation, Syracuse, New York,
for his assistance in preparing this book.

ISBN 0-590-48077-4

12 11 10 9 8 7 6 5 4 3 2 1   5 6 7 8 9/9

Printed in the U.S.A.   09

First Scholastic printing, February 1995

Electricity:

- lights our lamps.
- warms our heaters.
- spins our fans.
- moves our trains.
- carries our voices over telephone wires.
- brings us sound and pictures on TV.
- runs our computers.

But what is electricity?
We can't see it.
We can't hear it.
We can't smell it.

Electricity is a form of energy.
Energy is the ability to do work.

The energy in our muscles lets us walk,
talk, eat, and play.
The energy of jet engines speeds airplanes
through the air.
The energy of wind turns windmills
and pushes sailboats.
The energy of windup toys makes them move.

Electrical energy comes from electric generators.
Generators are machines that produce electricity.
You can make your own electric generator.
It's easy.

DO IT YOURSELF

Make an Electric Generator

Collect:

- a piece of electrical wire about two yards long.
- a bar magnet.
- a compass.

Ask an adult to peel one inch of covering off both
ends of the wire.
Wrap one end of the wire around your hand
about ten times to form a coil.
Slide the wire off your hand.

Wrap the other end of the wire
around the compass about five times.
Leave the wire there.
Twist the two metal ends of the wire together.

Now slide the magnet quickly back and forth
inside the coil.
This makes electricity flow in the wire.
You have made an electric generator!

Look at the compass.
Is the needle moving?

The moving needle tells you that electricity
is flowing through the wire.
This is how it works.
The wire is made up of billions and billions
of tiny bits.
These bits are called atoms.

Atoms are much too small to be seen.
But inside each atom are even smaller bits.
They are called electrons.
The electrons spin around the atom's center.

Sometimes the electrons move from one atom
to another atom.
Moving electrons produce a current of electricity.
When electrons move through the wire,
electricity flows through that wire.

Moving a magnet near wire sends the electrons
from atom to atom.
That's why electricity flowed from your tiny generator.
But only a little electricity came from your generator.
A powerful flow of electricity comes from the giant
generators of electric companies.

Giant generators have huge coils and magnets.
In most generators the magnet spins inside the coils.
In some generators coils spin inside a magnet.

The power for your tiny generator came
from muscles in your arm.
The power for most giant generators comes
from burning fuel.

The burning fuel heats water.
The water changes into steam.
The steam pressure spins the magnet in the generator.

The electricity from the giant generators goes into big wires.
These wires run along the tops of tall poles.
In some cities the wires are under the ground.
The electricity travels through these wires for many miles.

The long wires have short branches.
They bring electricity to homes, schools, stores, and other places.
One of these wires goes to your home.

Inside your house are electrical wires.
The wires bring electricity to everything
that needs it.
Lights on the ceilings and walls use electricity.
These lights are called fixtures.

Appliances in the home use electricity, too.
Appliances have wires with plugs.
The plugs fit into outlets in the wall.
Some common home appliances are:

- refrigerator, microwave, and dishwasher.
- radio, TV, and computer.
- lamps, fans, and heaters.
- toaster, blender, and coffee pot.
- clock, iron, and air conditioner.

The electricity that comes into your house
is very powerful.
It is also dangerous.
It can give you a severe shock.
So be careful around electrical fixtures and appliances.

You can check your home for electrical safety.

DO IT YOURSELF

Be an Electric Detective

Take a walk around your house.
Look for signs of danger.
Look—but don't touch!

1. Fixtures that don't work.
2. Broken appliances.
3. Torn or frayed electric wires.
4. Three or more appliances plugged into one outlet.
5. Outlets without safety covers.
6. People unplugging appliances by pulling the wire, not the plug.
7. People leaving lights or TV on when not in the room.

We plug appliances into electrical outlets.
But what if we want to carry a flashlight outdoors?
Then we use a battery to give us the electricity we need.

Would you like to make a battery?

DO IT YOURSELF

Make a Battery

Collect:

- a soup bowl half filled with water.
- about four tablespoons of table salt.
- a paper supermarket bag.
- a can of scouring powder.
- five shiny pennies.
- five shiny nickels.

Pour the salt into the water and stir.
Cut out nine one-inch squares of the paper bag.
Soak the squares in the salt water.

Hold the pennies and nickels under warm tap water.
Scrub both sides of each coin with scouring powder.
Rinse the coins in tap water.

Make a stack of coins and paper:
   nickel—wet paper
   penny—wet paper
   nickel—wet paper
   and so on.

The coins and wet paper work like a battery.
They produce a small flow of electricity.

Dip your fingers in the salt water.
Hold the stack with your thumb at the bottom
and pointer finger at the top.
Do you feel a tingling?
That's a very mild electric shock.

The mild electric shock comes from the battery.
It makes electricity just like the generator.
The electrons speed from atom to atom.
This form of electricity is called current electricity.

There is another kind of electricity.
It's called static electricity.
In static electricity the electrons don't flow
from atom to atom.
They just get knocked off some atoms.

DO IT YOURSELF

Shock Your Friends

Slide your feet on a rug or carpet.
(This works best if it's a cold, dry day.)
Now touch a friend's hand.
You'll both feel a mild electrical shock.

Sliding on the rug knocks electrons off some
atoms in your body.
It gives your body a charge of static electricity.
Touching your friend lets the electricity jump
from you to your friend.

You can do some fun tricks with static electricity.

DO IT YOURSELF

Electrical Balloons

Blow up a balloon.
Rub it quickly and lightly against something
made of wool.

- a woolen sweater, skirt, or trousers.
- woolen gloves, scarf, or socks.

The rubbing gives the balloon a charge
of static electricity.

Now hold the balloon against a wall.
The balloon sticks there!
It's static electricity at work.

Again, rub the balloon against wool to give it
an electrical charge.
Hold the balloon over someone's head.
Does the person's hair stand up?
It's static electricity at work again.

Next blow up two balloons.
Tie a string to each one.
Rub the balloons with wool.
Now they both have a charge.

Hold the end of each string.
Try to bring the two balloons together.
Can you do it?
No!
The static electricity pushes them away from each other.

You can do other static electricity tricks with a comb.
Try these.

DO IT YOURSELF

An Electrical Comb

All you'll need are:

- a tissue torn into very tiny bits.
- a handful of dry puffed cereal.
- a clean pocket comb.

Hold the comb with your fingertips.
Rub it on something made of wool,
or run it through your hair a few times.

Quickly pass the comb over the torn-up tissue.
What happens?
The paper bits jump up and stick to the comb.
It's static electricity at work.

Wait a few seconds.
The electrical charge starts to grow weak.
The bits of tissue fall off.

Try this experiment again with dry puffed cereal
instead of tissue.

You made static electricity by rubbing with wool.
The static electricity pulled things together.
And it pushed them apart.

You can even use static electricity to make a tiny
spark of electricity.
The spark is very weak.
It can't hurt you.
But this spark is like a tiny, tiny bolt of lightning!

BOOM!

☆
SNAP

DO IT YOURSELF

Make Lightning

This activity will only work on a cold, dry day.
In a dark room rub a comb with a piece of wool.
Quickly hold the end of the comb to a metal doorknob.

What do you see?
A small spark jumps between the comb
and the doorknob.
This is something like lightning.

What do you hear?
A crackling sound.
This is something like thunder.

☆ POP!

Crackle!
☆

SNAP!

Real lightning is a giant spark.
No one is sure what causes the spark of lightning.
They know it mostly comes on hot, humid days.
On some days a big, dark thundercloud forms
in the sky.
Drops of water and bits of ice are in the cloud.

Winds in the cloud blow the water and ice up
and down.
They rub against each other.
It is like you rubbing a comb with wool.
The electrons are knocked out of the atoms.
The charge of static electricity grows bigger
and bigger.

Then, suddenly, a giant spark flashes across the sky.
That's the bolt of lightning.
Lightning can jump between a cloud and earth.
Or it can jump between two clouds.

After you see the lightning, you hear the thunder.
The lightning makes the thunder.

A lightning bolt is very, very hot.
It quickly heats the air it passes through.

The heated air explodes out in all directions.
Thunder is the sound of the exploding air.

The static electricity you make at home is safe.
But lightning is very dangerous.
If you are outdoors when lightning flashes:

- go into a house or automobile.
- don't stand near a tall tree or pole.
- crouch down in an open field.
- don't go near water.
- don't touch anything made of metal.

If you are indoors:

- stay away from doors and windows.
- stay away from sinks and tubs
- don't use electrical appliances.
- only use the phone in an emergency.

Current electricity is also dangerous.
But you'll be safe if you are careful.
And you'll enjoy all the wonders of electricity!